ENGLISH

N

China

China Through the Eyes of Forest L. Littke

AuthorHouse™
1663 Liberty Drive
Bloomington, IN 47403
www.authorhouse.com
Phone: 1 (800) 839-8640

Published by AuthorHouse 11/30/2016

ISBN: 978-1-5049-6158-5 (sc)
ISBN: 978-1-5049-6160-8 (hc)
ISBN: 978-1-5049-6159-2 (e)

Library of Congress Control Number: 2015920018

Print information available on the last page.

authorHOUSE®

ENGLISH
N
China

China Through the Eyes of Forest L. Littke

FOREST L. LITTKE

Preface

English n China.....or Oddities n China
拼写错误在英语ie: written mistake in English

China through the eyes of Forest Littke

Wikipedia says...''The English word Chinglish is a portmanteau of Chinese and English. The Chinese equivalent is ZHONGSHI YINGYU (中式英语) or "Chinese style English". However, this is not a close look at the way Chinese is translated into written English as the written form or idea is in the wrong word order creating a mixture or upset of thought. It is, however, a collection of my "snapshots" of the oddities that I have uncovered as I live in China. In recent years, because of the "smart phone" or the "tablet or Ipad", people are now spending all their time texting or playing games when traveling from A to B. They have stopped "smelling the roses" so to speak and so I do take the time to look around me and catch the majesty of the simple things along the way! Life is too short not to! Do you agree with me, with this rational?

In 2010, I was working as a Foreign Language teacher in Shandong, Dezhou. My colleague and I where heading toward the gym and waiting for the elevator when I noticed the sign in front of me which would read "in case of fife please take the stairs". I said out loud "fife! Oh they mean Fire". We both laughed at the mistake and continued on our way to the gym. Since that moment, I have noticed many such oddities or "mistakes" and began a casual hobby of collecting these for two purposes. The first is to share with others for the purpose of humor as it should put a smile on your face. The second reason is to share with the English speaking world and general public about the Chinese Culture and their constant hunger to adapt to and use the English language within a Chinese setting. China has become my second home as I have lived here since 2010. I have taught and educated thousands of students both in a College and University settings, have tutored privately (面对面) "face to face" and have taught in English "summer boot camps". Now my aim is to have the largest collection of photos of English mistakes in a Chinese setting of any person in the world. This book intends to go the extra mile and captures the spelling MISTAKES in a photo setting and with a commentary to support it. Thus giving the average English person a reason to smile when they see it. Most commentaries will also have the location of where I found the ERROR, so it will end up as a type of travel guide so you can see it for your self while your traveling through China. Occasionally you will be told about a particular theme such as "garbage cans" or "Christmas". Other times their will be no theme just random words which have been "twisted" as I find them.

It should be noted as well, that for all the critics who will question the validity or need for a book such as this book, remember two things. I am showing culture differences with a touch of humor. The original Chinglish as taught in the Chinese education system is about a particular way to express a thought which is CONTRARY to the normal English routine. Later issues only look at a brief sample of Chinese style English which is usually in paragraph form and is difficult to photograph. Such as the back of a car window which has a display!So I will choose samples cautiously. The bulk of my collection of photographs is with the individual word that creates all the fuss among us who know the difference. As a Canadian, I reserve the right to poke fun at something that is out of the ordinary and to simply put a smile on YOUR face and show you the twisted English that I have discovered in my travels. Take it with you on the bus or subway, take it with you on your vacation whether it be in or out side of China. Use it in the classroom for conversation perspective as an "ice-breaker" or use it just for casual reading because it does not require a PhD back ground. My goal is to have the largest collection of anyone else.

As a closing remark to the beginning of this, my first book, I wish to say that I have missed many opportunities of catching a good "snap shot" of a caption. On the way to Wuhan airport this summer, after passing the toll both in my taxi, I read a sign which reads "Bnckle up" rather then Buckle up. So their are missed chances due to poor conditions! Dozens may one day turn to hundreds of lost chances.

Before you begin, I challenge you to look at the photo first to try and decipher the problem prior to reading the commentary ... then, prepare to enjoy it!

Forest L. Littke

P.s. I have included site maps to show you the general areas where I have traveled and found the displays.

CHRISTMAS IN CHINA

The idea of Christmas within "New age" communist China is a fairly new concept. Some times Santa Clause is referred to as "Old man Christmas". During my summer boot camp this year (2015) I asked my adult students about the name "Santa Claus" and they all shook their heads saying "we do not know these words"! They do put up trees, they do decorate the tree, but there are no gifts placed under the tree. The concept of gift giving at Christmas time is still foreign to them.

My first Christmas in China and the succeeding years since, I have noticed something that we do not experience back home. You can hear Christmas music year round in the malls and the Christmas posters are never taken down...they stay up year round! The idea that the Festival ends on December 31 st does not exist!

You can see a variety of Posters in this first book. Enjoy!

Wuhan, Wuchang district:

In Wuhan I find "christmac" instead of "Christmas". I found it posted at the local gym that I attend. In the Chinese language there is no such thing as "Capitalization" for any word at the beginning of a sentence or for any noun....so in this case "Christmas" will a small "C" is the result.

Wuhan, Wuchang district:

On my campus of 湖北第二师范学院,(Hubei 2nd Normal University) the graffiti says "Marry" instead of "merry".

The reverse of English with "merry" following Christmas. There are many such rules in Chinese!

Just a new style of writing "merry". They can be a very creative people with Western ideas.

Wuhan, Wuchang district:

In Chinese it says Merry Christmas ...圣诞快乐. (sheng dan kuai le) "Holy birth happy " is how the Chinese say it. If for example you where to wish some one a "happy birthday"...the word order is in reverse to English... Ie:birthday happy! Sheng re kuai le

Wuhan, Wuchang district: In Guanggu, a near by shopping center window...I think the missing "Y" is simple case of wear and tear.

...but this does have the missing "y" and the missing "C"

No mistake really just a new twist that caught my eye. The Chinese are very open to the concept of Christmas but miss the idea of the giving of gifts as yet.

I share this photo only because of its location. Wuhan at Guang gu business center is hit with perhaps a million people during a busy day even near Christmas time. Thousands of shops are located on basement floor levels. This shop is located in a little corner off the beaten path where perhaps 100 people may slip past. Who ever drew it on the window did a beautiful job with no mistakes. However, the people who traffic this area seldom speak or read any English other then "hello or goodbye". I saw the display and snapped it because it was so nicely done in comparison to the other "oops!" displayed around town.

Last but certainly not the least is this Spanish poster which was found at a Christmas party in Wuhan in 2014.

It is very odd because the main foreign languages taught are English, Japanese and some French.

定点等候，定时出发

Englsih Guided Tour by Volunteers
Available at variable time
See schedule below

免费讲解时间
Schedule of guided tours (all free)

Suzhou-Jiangsu province

Jiangsu province is a stone throw from Shanghai in the East of China.

My trip to Suzhou I found this on one of my tours "Englsih"

outhern Yangzi River delta r
lopment growthe of Chinese
ral resources and commercia
into a flourishing and prospe
d literati who settled in this

More Suzhou, I found "growthe" on the same tour

ecame so adept at emulating tl

om the facsimile. These highly

nterest to dstablish new standa

ly manipulate the art marketpla

zitan and huanghuali woods an

nental items, they favored ancien

Same tour..."dstablish" should be establish.

aterials like zitan and hua

ss. For ornamental items, t

ties. As tren dsetters for th

the public to eagerly, and so

Ming Jiaqing, Longqing and

"tren dsetters" should be "trend setters"

ntry, they advocated n
, follow. This was especia
hen the valus of collectib

"valus" aught to be "values"

FIREEXTINGUISHERBOX

Random eyes catchers

While traveling the subway I found "fireextinguisherbox", they forget
to put spaces between the words....fire extinguisher box! In the Chinese
language, they do not use spaces between the characters as we do.

Wuhan, Wuchang district: the missing "L" in professional, I believe is more wear and tear.

On the high speed train from Yichang to Wuhan I found "whe chair" in Chinese the sign is correct meaning "wheel chair"

In Wuhan at Guanggu traffic circle I found "bolanlcal" rather than BOTANICAL. You will notice as well that they criss-cross languages. So they will use the Chinese sound then add the English word next.

At the Wuhan high speed train station..."inquries" rather than INQUIRIES at the customer service booth.

One man's trash is another man's TREASURE!

I feel that I may be the ONLY person who takes and interest in Garbage cans! One man's trash is another man's cash......so to speak!

Hebei, Baoding: Baoding is a small town south of Beijing....."recep
tacle" rather than RECEPTACLE as they continue to forget
the spacing. In Chinese these do not space words!

不可回收
Organism

山西省万荣县裴庄环卫
器材厂
手机: 013703591078 电话: 0359-4593039

I thought this was interesting as they chose a word not common
in this way. "organism" was found in Baoding.

Hubei, Yichang: "waster".... So funny in my opinion. Yichang is famous for the 3 gorges damn in China. By tour bus, it is at least one hour drive away from the city of Yichang. Very beautiful in the summer or autumn but terrible in the winter months because of the heavy rain that it receives.

Wuhan: "marine dancer"....got to be careful about those dancer's.

In Baoding...a simple case of oops!"Noe-recyclable". NOT-RECYLABLE

This is another classic case of Chinglish "recyclablf". I had to look closely at this one and was an "f" instead of an "E" that was robbed off.

On a trip to Yichang of the "three gorges fame", we find "wast" instead of WASTE.

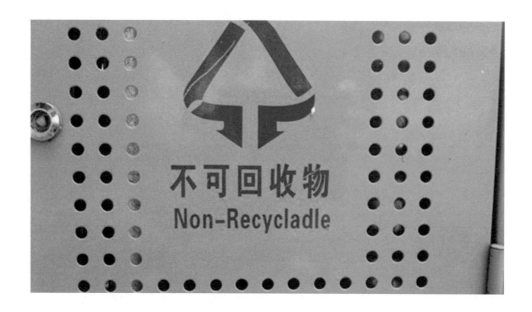

A classic case....”recycladle” instead of RECYCABLE.

中国光谷

ptics alley of hina

Wuhan: Oops! The printer did not get it quite right..... I saw several boxes and the “O,V and the C” are all over the place. Look at these next ones closely.

Same printer error.....continues!

Wuhan: But on this one......They tried to use black on black and this was their result. I saw dozens that day and they all had the same problem..."ptics, alley of hina" instead of OPTICS VALLEY OF CHINA. Later, I found that the missing color was RED on black.

Walking the streets of Baoding....."new the fall" instead of NEW THIS FALL.

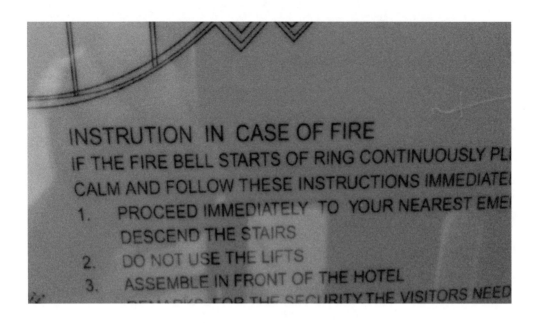

The Town of Baoding

A Baoding hotel, again just south of Beijing. The following caught my attention. In my hotel I found "instrution" instead of INSTRUCTION. Also the grammar word "of" should be OFF! Or "of" could be "to"....bell starts to ring.

In the near by super market in Baoding..."drovide". I think they mean PROVIDE.

**One of my personal favorites is this one........So, we are
not considered Foreigners but ALEINS. Haha**

**This beats them all, also in Baoding. "LWE COME", I showed the
shop owner the mistake and told her it should be WELCOME!
Ah 对我懂, (dui wo dong) "yes i understand".**

Hebei, Baoding: "propreties" instead of PROPERTIES. When
I type fast, this happens to me, but this is a business!

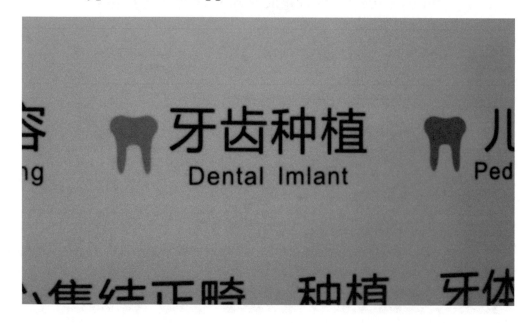

Wuhan. It has been my home since 2013 and so the collection grows.

On a visit to my dentist to get a new crown. I discovered
"Imlant" rather than IMPLANT.

Hebei, Baoding: The final one on my visit in Baoding...."electrcl" instead of ELECTRICAL.

Hubei, Wuhan: Same mall....."smokeng" smoking. One thing I will mention here about the culture. They have signs up everywhere about no smoking. But still, in the restaurants and even in the toilets, they lite up like chimneys. Their is no one to enforce the rule.

Hubei, Wuhan: A hair salon at Guanggu..."closer tostylists, closertohair". I disagree unless it was deliberate labeling. CLOSER TO STYLISTS. CLOSER TO HAIR, but it could be a marketing ploy. As I noted earlier....they fail to put spaces between the words!

Wuchang district of Wuhan: "restalirant"vs RESTAURANT.

In Wuhan, I love this one, found it while having lunch with my girlfriend. "smok-free" vs SMOKE-FREE.

America has Silicon Valley, Wuhan has "opllcs valley" vs OPTICS VALLEY.

中船重工第七一九研究所
719th Reseach Institute Of China Shipbuilding
Industry Corporation
锦江之星、百时快捷武昌火车站店
Jinjiang Inn Wuchang Railway Station

Wuhan, wuchang district: On the subway system in ..."reseach" vs RESEARCH.

高压室
HV COMP ART

**"comp art" ... It means COMPARTMENT. HV here means High Pressure,
but they often use the "V"letter to describe the sound they wish to make.**

My new crown came in this box. "customerized" vs CUSTOMIZED。

Hubei, Wuhan: I was walking out of a store and found this advertized, "eechnician".....is supposed to be ELECTRICIAN. At first glance, I thought "electrician", however, the Chinese script written above it gives a more decisive description. Hence "technician". However, there is a twist in the above Chinese.... old versus simplified. In this example, the second and fourth characters do not look the same as " 技术人员"(ji shu ren yuan). Today's students must learn both styles of characters. The meaning is identical. So, a foreign person must adapt and know about both to comprehend Chinese properly. On any tv program in China, the script on the bottom of the tv will use the OLD script in order to accommodate the pre 1949 generation. When at a museum etc, you will see the same results. So, as with the above sign, both scripts are converged. Today, all students in modern China, writing any articles must write in "simplified" form.

At the HanKou train station in Wuhan…"POLIcE" looks just a little off here.

Hubei, Wuhan: HanKou railway station has…."LET"……
is the very short form of TOILET or 厕所.

Means wet floor...."careful not to slide". You will find this sign in many restaurants in China.

No is does not mean "goon"! They are trying to say GO ON for when you board the subway train haha. 乘车 (cheng che) means "to ride".

Hubei, Wuhan: "hote" this sign is telling you where the local HOTEL is.

Wuhan: "no tooting" is their way of saying NO HORNES allowed.

Please note that their is no speed posted on the sign.

Wuhan, Wuchang district: "wain" instead of MAIN.

wuhan: "lo" instead of the normal LOT. Maybe the T just fell off. The Chinese word just above "parking" also is missing the bottom portion. There are maybe 20 signs in total in this parking lot....almost all have something wrong with them.

Wuhan, Wuchang district: 生活厂场...... **Is better translated as PUBLIC SQUARE.**

Wuhan.Wuchang district: "Gnangshan" here is wrong, the use of PinYin is how the Chinese create the English sound for Chinese. However the word should be written as GUANGSHAN. They turned the U upside down by mistake and glued it in as a "n" instead of the proper letter "u".

Wuhan, Wuchang district: the "o" looks a little lonely with out the "f".

Wuhan, Wuchang district: The "T" is missing for LOT.

Wuhan, Wuchang district: CN I believe is the short form for CENTURY. 二十一世纪 would make it 21 st century!

(warning dancer!)

Wuhan, Wuchang district: I found the "dancer" at a work site early one morning while out having a morning walk.

Wuhan, Wuchang district: "fire nose" should be FIRE HOSE.
Maybe you could argue that it could also be the nose, but
later you will find many that say hose on them!

It is all about spacing in English.....so HEALTH should not be
separated. 健康 means healthy and does not mean heal!

Wuhan, Wuchang district: the "N" now is glued to look like a "z" and the word should be separated to be CHINA WELFARE LOTTERY. The Chinese do spend a lot of time in these places hoping to WIN the big prise.

Guanggu shopping center in Wuhan: "sirce" instead of SINCE.

Just clumsy spacing when making the sign.

if you can not do it with ONE sign, then do it with TWO SIGNS!

We can argue about this one, but I will still say it is a spacing issue!

"mulnicipal" rather than MUNICIPAL. Remember that this is
an advertisement by both the Province as well as the city!

This sign is just a few minutes North of my school. "calley" instead of VALLEY. The sun was going down quickly, so it was hard to get clear shot of the sign. So look closely!

Wuhan "the city" is divided in to three seperate districts. HanKou, HanYang and WuChang. WuChang in the South East has countless parks and little lakes in the city. So I was with a friend when I came across this one. "wate" instead of WATER

址:湖北省武汉经济技术开发区民营科技工业园E栋三楼
l:3rd Floor,EBuilding,Non-Govermental SCL-TECH industry Garden
(STIG),WuHan Economy&technological Development Zone,hubei Pr
话Tel：027-84222666　售后服务customer service：027-
真Fax：027-84295722　邮箱Email:webmaster@jgq-mgy
止Web:www.jgqyc.com　　邮编PS:430056

Can you spot the problems? "E building", Governmental, economy & technological.

You will probably feel I am just being fussy! "ra i lway" again is a spacing issue.
When you are grading papers, you have to point out the little things to the students.

Wuhan subway station: "fir extinguisher".......FIRE EXTINGUISHER. I strongly believe that some one may have rubbed off the "E", but it strictly speculation on my part!. But their way of writing "stop fire" really does catch my eye! 灭火 (mie huo) means "extinguish fire".

So the logic behind the character is very exact as in this expression.

"not export" is supposed to mean NO EXIT. The place where I buy most of my stuff in Wuhan at the Guanggu business center.

"tivcketing"......TICKETING at Hankou train station in Wuhan. Their are three train stations in Wuhan. Hankou is in the North West, Wuhan station is in the far East and Wuchang is in the South district. 6 months later, I returned to this location and the sign had been removed and corrected.

Wuhan, Wuchang district: "spotting".......SPITTING
at the Buddhist temple BAO TONG SI

GuangDong, Shenzhen: "aera"....AREA at the ShenZhen North
train station. Was in a rush that day....not a clear photo!

Guangdong, Shenzhen: "restauran" .....RESTAURANT
in south Shenzhen in 国贸 (guo mao) area.

Guangdong, Shenzhen: "spokesperon" .... SPOKESPERSON
in the same "KingGlory"building.

Guangdong, ShenZhen: "cirlce".... CIRCLE near
my Vienna hotel in Guo Mao area.

GuangDong, Shenzhen: In my hotel. "somke"....SMOKE. They do push safety in the hotels, but never had the English proof-read. I took several photos, but the camera would always blur up because the writing was so small. This was my best shot!

Guangdong, ShenZhen: In the Vienna hotel, "protecl"..... PROTECT. China is known for its polluted air and water. You never ever drink the tap-faucet water! Always boil it first unless they provide bottled water for the room. But they always encourage YOU to save water where possible and avoid needless washing. Chinese as a people are "clean freaks" so to speak.

源根部紧压手柄，约剂即会喷出。

Instructions:
In case of fire,put out safety pin,
aim nozzle at the basic of fire within
the effective range,press the handle
and extinguish forward.

火警电话：**110**

**Guangdong, Shenzhen: Vienna hotel, "put"... PULL, "basic"...
BASE. As well they do not put a space after the commas.**

单/双号
Single/double numder

**Guangdong, ShenZhen:Vienna hotel,"numder"....NUMBER. 单 "shan"
does mean single, as well 双 "shuang" does mean double. 号 "hao"
does mean number. But NUMDER does not work in this case!**

GuangDong, Shenzhen: It is written here as "ank", however I feel it was a product of wear and tear and the B just got removed. As an additional note, I took this photo by shooting on the side. In ancient China it was customary to write the language from Top to Bottom.....Left side of paper to the Right side. At the time of the Great Revolution of Mao the people began to write from the left to the right and in a horizontal format rather than vertical. When you travel to China and visit the Old monuments.....it reads from "right to left"! On behalf of languages in general, English is one of the more recent languages to emerge in our species history. Languages which include Chinese, and other ancient cultures all wrote from Left to Right.

Guangdong, Shenzhen: Friendship Hotel:"dail"........
DIAL. These simple things put a smile on my face!

Gaungdong, ShenZhen: "subwav" .... SUBWAY. Often, if I have nothing urgent
to do or see while in a city, I will walk casually just glancing and searching
for anomalies.So I capture what the average person will simply ignore!

Guangdong,Shenzhen: "vahicle occess".......VEHICLE ACCESS. I pointed this
sign out to several of my Shenzhen friends who work as professional translators.
After spending a moment looking and thinking, they would ask. "So what is wrong
with it?" When I point out the mistake, they always say...."You have a good eye!"

Guangdong,ShenZhen: At a Vienna hotel, "piease"......PLEASE.

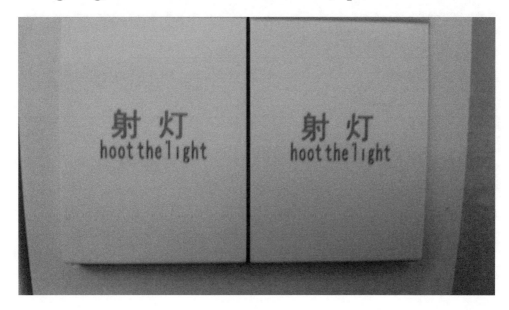

Guangdong, Shenzhen: Same hotel Vienna in ShenZhen: "hoot"! 射灯 means SPOT LIGHT so it becomes true Chinglish with this combination.

Guangdong, Shenzhen: "extinguisheer" for EXTINGUISHER at Shenzhen market.

Location possibly Hebei, Handan! It is a small town near Beijing, "hlep..........
HELP. The lighting conditions in the hotel hall was very poor!

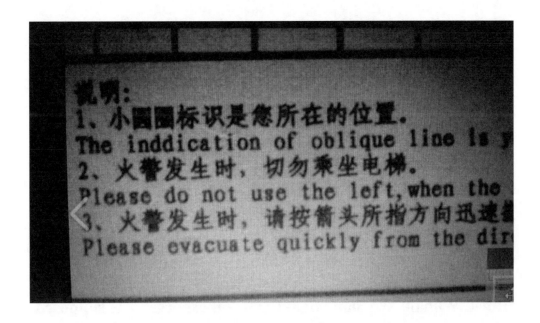

Location, possibly Changsha in South China. 1. "inddication" instead of INDICATION. 2 "left"..... Is supposed to be the LIFT or ELEVATOR.

Hubei, Wuhan, Wuchang district: Baotongsi TEMPLE. "I S LAND" or ISLAND.

Hubei, Wuhan, Wuchang district:"Clotheshorse"... Is supposed to be CLOTHES HANGER. In the local Walmart store. Did you know that every foreign store that wants to open in China must give 51% owner ship to the Chinese Government! True.

Hubei, Wuhan, Wuchang district: "fire Wuhan: figting"......fire-fighting.

Hubei, Wuhan: "magicalfall".... MAGICAL FALL, spacing spacing spacing. These types of signs can be seen in any city and province in China. It could be a simple case of "branding" which I deal with in later issues.

Hubei,Wuhan, Wuchang district: "civing"........GIVING. I am puzzled as to why they do not proof read before making it public! This is a small ladies boutique shop.

To be continued .... With volume 2

....a map of each province and city visited will be displayed in each volume for your convenience and pleasure.

 China as a country.

Hubei province,Wuhan and Yichang city.

Guangdong province, ShenZhen city

JiangSu province, Suzhou city

Hebei province, Baoding and Handan

Special mention must be given to 孙兆玲 "Lily", she was the Chinese lady who suggested that I collect my photos and put them into a book form. Without her input (pushing) this book would never have occurred. Her friends call her Ling (玲) and I owe much to her.

Special mention to my student 李宁悦 "Honey"for creating my maps.

"Honey" is one of my students who is majoring in Business English.

* all photos have been taken personally by the author and are the property of the author. Any reproduction of, or part thereof for commercial gain is strictly prohibited without written consent.

*QQ International:1523646290

*WeChat: Forest1959:15171484933

Printed in the United States
By Bookmasters